border to border · teen to teen · border to border · teen to teen · border to border

Teens in

EGYPT

by Barbara A. Somervill

Content Adviser: Christopher Rose, M.A.,
Outreach Coordinator, Center for Middle Eastern Studies,
University of Texas at Austin

Reading Adviser: Katie Van Sluys, Ph.D.,
Department of Teacher Education,
DePaul University

Compass Point Books ◆ Minneapolis, Minnesota

Compass Point Books
3109 West 50th Street, #115
Minneapolis, MN 55410

Editor: Julie Gassman
Designers: The Design Lab and Jaime Martens
Page Production: Bobbie Nuytten
Photo Researcher: Eric Gohl
Cartographer: XNR Productions, Inc.
Library Consultant: Kathleen Baxter

Art Director: Jaime Martens
Creative Director: Keith Griffin
Editorial Director: Nick Healy
Managing Editor: Catherine Neitge

The author wishes to thank Osman Aboul-Nasr for his assistance in writing this book.

Library of Congress Cataloging-in-Publication Data
Somervill, Barbara A.
   Teens in Egypt / by Barbara A. Somervill.
      p. cm. — (Global connections)
   Includes bibliographical references and index.
   ISBN-13: 978-0-7565-3294-9 (library binding)
   ISBN-10: 0-7565-3294-9 (library binding)
   1. Teenagers—Egypt—Juvenile literature. 2. Youth—Egypt—Social conditions—Juvenile
literature. I. Title. II. Series.
   HQ799.E3S66 2008
   305.2350962—dc22   2007003938

Visit Compass Point Books on the Internet at *www.compasspointbooks.com*
or e-mail your request to *custserv@compasspointbooks.com*

Table of Contents

Cairo ★

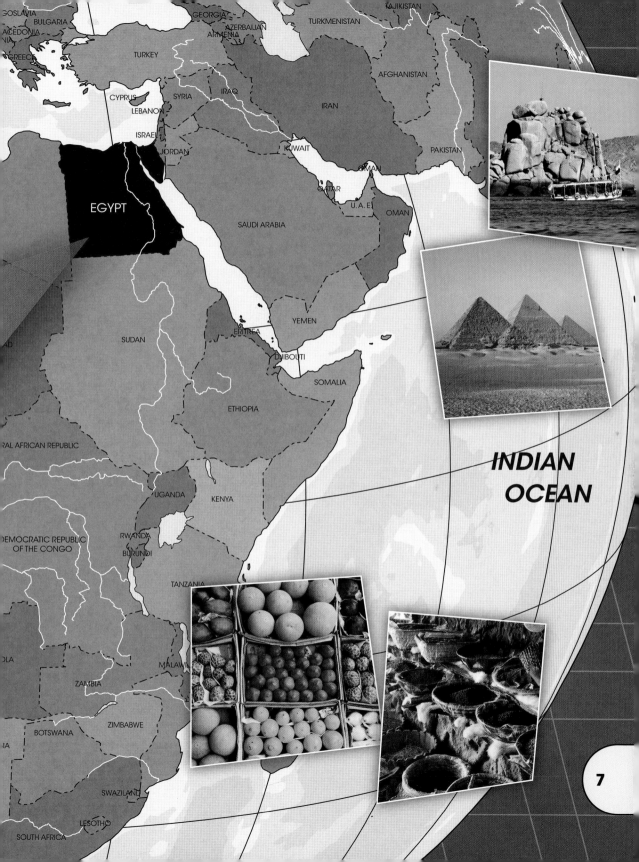

GOSLAVIA
BULGARIA
ACEDONIA
NIA
GREECE

TURKEY

CYPRUS
LEBANON
ISRAEL
JORDAN

EGYPT

GEORGIA
ARMENIA
AZERBAIJAN

SYRIA

IRAQ

KUWAIT

QATAR
U. A. E

SAUDI ARABIA

TURKMENISTAN

IRAN

OMAN

OMAN

AFGHANISTAN

PAKISTAN

AL AFRICAN REPUBLIC

SUDAN

ERITREA
DJIBOUTI

YEMEN

SOMALIA

ETHIOPIA

AD

UGANDA

RWANDA
BURUNDI

KENYA

DEMOCRATIC REPUBLIC
OF THE CONGO

TANZANIA

INDIAN
OCEAN

OLA

MALAWI

ZAMBIA

ZIMBABWE

BOTSWANA

IA

SWAZILAND

LESOTHO

SOUTH AFRICA

7

IT IS SATURDAY MORNING IN EGYPT, AND MANY CITY TEENS ARE IN SCHOOL. Other students have the day off, and for them, Saturday is for practicing soccer, heading to the mall, or doing homework. Some teens go to work. They sell spices in the market or guard parked cars for money. Still other teens are needed to help in their homes. They bake bread, care for brothers and sisters, or wash clothes.

In the rural regions, teenage boys might cast fishing nets in the Nile or pick cotton in the fields. A 13-year-old girl feeds her family's chickens or goats; her 16-year-old sister plans her wedding, which is coming up in three weeks. Teenagers make up 20 percent of Egypt's population. In a country steeped in ancient history, its teens balance the old and the new. They are Egypt's future.

Eighty-three percent of secondary school-aged girls are enrolled in school, compared to 88 percent of boys.

CHAPTER ONE

It's All About Exams

AROUND THE WORLD, TEENS DEAL WITH FAMILY, FRIENDS, AND SCHOOL EVERY DAY. In Egypt, education takes up a major part of many teens' lives. Parents expect their children to work hard and get good grades. Sounds familiar, doesn't it?

Egyptian schools are based on the British system of education because Great Britain once ruled Egypt. The British opened English-style schools there, and that system remains. Teens stay in the same classroom all day, while the teachers move from class to class.

Boys and girls attend different schools and usually wear uniforms. Boys wear pants, white shirts, and ties. During winter months, a blazer is added to the outfit. Girls wear the same style of uniforms, with long skirts in place of pants. Muslim girls may choose to wear head-scarves in accordance with their religion. Away from school the classic teen "uniform" of jeans, T-shirts, and sneakers has Egyptian students looking just like teens all over the world.

Three levels of schooling make up the Egyptian school system: primary, preparatory, and secondary. The first two levels are considered basic education, while the third level helps prepare a student for university, a skilled trade, or a job. Public education is free.

Egyptian children begin school at age 6. Primary school (ages 6 to 12) covers the basic subjects: reading and writing Arabic, math, science, and arts. Boys and girls at this level can be in the same classroom.

Most primary school children

Teen Scenes

Two 18-year-old boys write down their math homework assignment and take out their books for their English lesson. They are both in their last year of secondary school in Cairo. They have been studying for months so they can pass their review exams. Like many Egyptian students with wealthy parents, the boys work with a tutor every afternoon.

In the city, a young woman straightens up the fabrics on display in her family's street market stall. There will be no university in her future. She had to leave school at age 14 to work. Yet, she is better off than her mother, who started working at age 10. Her grandmother never went to school at all.

Farther up the Nile near Aswan, a teen boy checks on the water levels of his plants in the vocational school lab. He is studying agricultural technology— the science side of farming. He hopes to learn how to increase the crop yield of his family's cotton farm.

These teens will follow very different paths. Education for the wealthy leads to making more wealth. Low- or middle-income teens will probably remain in the economic level to which they were born. There are few rags-to-riches success stories in Egypt.

begin learning English in their first year. It is a holdover from the days of British rule, but learning English also prepares students for dealing with the outside world. Ninety-three percent of children eligible for school attend the first year. One-fourth of those students will drop out before their sixth year. Most dropouts are girls forced to leave school to work at home to help their families.

Primary school attendance is required by law. The attendance rate for girls is 82 percent for primary schools. But this does not tell the whole story. In cities, nearly 98 percent of girls attend school. In rural areas, that percentage drops. In some poorer districts, only 15 to 20 percent of girls attend school. The problem is clear: Girls who do not attend school grow into women who cannot read and write. Illiteracy continues to be a major problem in Egypt, where more than 42 percent of individuals over age 15 cannot read.

There are still some cultural attitudes that discourage girls' education in rural areas. Some parents believe that Islamic teachings place little value

Many primary schools do not have desks. Students sit and listen from rows of chairs.

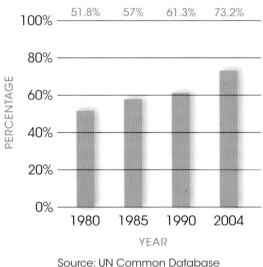

Youth Literacy Rate

Literacy among youth ages 15 to 24 is on its way up.

51.8%   57%   61.3%   73.2%

PERCENTAGE

100%
80%
60%
40%
20%
0%

1980   1985   1990   2004

YEAR

Source: UN Common Database

on girls' educa-
tion. Others do not like
the idea of boys and girls going to
school together.

However, the most common
reasons for low school attendance are
economic. Families in rural areas need
workers, not students. Farms need a
certain amount of work done each day
to keep them going, and children often
have to help out. In situations where
parents cannot afford to send all of their
children to school, boys usually get to
go to school and girls are kept home.

Rural
parents often
expect girls to
grow up, get married,
raise children, and keep
the household. Meanwhile,
boys will need to get a job and earn a
living to support their family. In rural
Egyptian culture, when girls marry, they
become part of their husband's family.
A son, however, brings his wife into his
family. Parents often educate their sons
because their futures are tied to the
family's future.

Education Reform

In 1995, the Education Innovations
Committee recommended sweeping
reforms of Egypt's public school system.

Eleven-year-old Doa'a Abdel-Hameed has never attended school. She spends her days fishing with her family on the Nile River.

High on the committee's "wish list" is increasing the overall enrollment of girls in schools. Retaining girls in both urban and rural schools is also important.

Rural school attendance for all students is a particular concern. The committee made changes that would allow both boys and girls to stay in school longer. One of those changes made the school schedule more flexible, which was essential for children of farming families. Even today, however, only 40 percent to 70 percent of rural children attend school, and most of them are boys. In some cases, only 12 girls for every 100 boys attend school.

School for All

Egypt celebrates Education for All (EFA) for a week each year. The goal is to have all children attending school by 2015. UNESCO (United Nations Educational, Scientific, and Cultural Organization) has worked with Egypt's government to increase the enrollment of girls in school. Pro-education posters are displayed on classroom walls, and essay and art contests are held to promote education for girls. Prizes are offered for top students and teachers in the poorest school districts. All girls who go to school in these areas receive certificates for attendance.

Lack of attendance is a serious problem, but so is overcrowding. Fifteen million students attend 38,000 schools. One-third of Egypt's schools have more than 40 students per classroom. And many have more than 60 students in one classroom. Classes are crowded, books are old, and teachers are under-trained and overwhelmed. But small steps are being made. Egypt built 800 new schools in 2005 and 2006 in an effort to control the overcrowding.

Education in Egypt continues to face major challenges. And the government's attempts at improving education are not always successful. Every time the government gets a new education minister, the plans for improved education change. Often programs are scrapped before they have a chance to work.

Also, access to technology is limited. Computer training is more of a dream than a reality. In recent years, a government program placed computers in many rural schools. As a result, many rural schools have more computers per student than city schools. But many students do not know how to use the computers, so they have no value. Teachers in these schools also may not know how to use the computers. In fact, many computers are never even taken out of their original delivery boxes.

The difference between rural and urban education is dramatic in Egypt, as is the difference between education for the upper- and lower-income families. Children of upper-income parents have

Modern, well-equipped schools are too expensive for most Egyptians.

computers in their homes, play video games, and learn with the help of private tutors. Children from low-income households must work to help feed their families.

Preparing for the Future

From 13 to 15 years of age, children attend preparatory school. Classes include Arabic, English, history, geography, science, math, and possibly French. In the British school system, French was always the foreign language taught in school, and it continues to be taught in Egyptian schools. School is only six hours a day, and because of

17

The government provides carpet schools where teens can learn a trade and earn a wage.

overcrowding, students often attend in shifts.

Secondary school is also a three-year program. Students can pursue either general studies or a vocational/technical education. General studies include science, math, languages, or arts. During the first year, students take a full range of subjects. Depending on their success, they may then follow a course of study in science, math, or a program called humanistic studies. Humanistic courses are connected to the arts and include languages, literature, fine art, and music.

Although the day is divided into eight class periods, the schedule varies from day to day. On Monday, a student might have two periods of English and no physical education. The next day might find double math sessions on the schedule.

The alternative to general studies is to take vocational and technical education programs. These schools provide students with skills and knowledge they can use in the workplace. Students may learn agriculture, construction trades, mechanical technology, or other job-related information. Technical schools are five-year programs. Vocational schools offer both three- and five-year plans, depending on the course of study.

A Bus Ride in Cairo

piastres
(pe-ASS-turz)

A group of teens is heading to school. At 10 to 25 *piastres* (U.S. 1 cent to 4 cents) per trip, bus travel in Cairo is cheap, but it challenges even a native Egyptian. There are no bus maps telling the routes, and bus stops are not well marked. This is the same bus system teens use to get to school. Most teens in Cairo know the bus system well and allow plenty of extra time to get to school.

Crowded streets in Cairo can make it difficult for buses to make their way.

19

Private School Education

Parents who can afford to do so might choose to send their children to a private school. Choosing a private school is a serious commitment. These schools are very expensive, costing 20,500 to 34,750 Egyptian pounds (U.S.$3,600 to $6,100). Add to that book fees, uniform costs, and other school-related expenses. The average family income in Egypt is about 39,250 Egyptian pounds (U.S.$6,875), so only a small percentage of parents can afford private schools for their children.

A full range of private schools is available in Cairo, Alexandria, and other large cities. These schools are often sponsored by religious groups, but they must still follow Egypt's national curriculum. Conditions in these schools may not be better than local public schools. Overcrowding, so evident in public schools, exists equally in private schools.

Many Muslim parents choose to send their children to an Islamic school. Together Egypt's Islamic schools make up the Azharite Education system. These schools provide a basic education with

Computer lessons are sometimes part of religious education.

Students at Islamic schools read from the Qur'an while seated on the floor.

major emphasis on reading and understanding the Qur'an and other Islamic studies. The Supreme Council of the Al-Azhar Institution selects the teachers and plans the curriculum. It also enforces strict Islamic codes of behavior in Azharite schools. About 4 percent of Egypt's students study in Islamic schools.

Throughout the 12 years of Islamic education, girls and boys are separated. Even 6-year-old girls have no contact with boys their own age in school. Upon graduation, these students may go to Al-Azhar University. The respected school is more than 1,000 years old. However, graduates of the Azharite program do not qualify for public universities. University admissions depend on following a standard curriculum, and many Islamic schools do not fully meet those standards.

Test Time

Regardless of the type of school attended, homework and exams play a dominant role in education. At the end of their third year, students take the *thanweyah a'mah,* a three-week required exam. The score they receive is critical. The opportunity to attend a college or university in Egypt depends on the scores earned. Universities do not consider past performance, extracurricular activities, or family situations. They simply look at the exam scores and make their decisions. Only students who score 94 percent or better are allowed to study medicine in university. A score of 91 percent may lead to math studies and a possible

future as an engineer. Students who receive high grades are not forced to become doctors or engineers. However, students with lower scores have no chance to pursue those careers.

The school year is long, and the summer holiday is shorter than in many other countries. Graduation comes at the end of the three-week exam period. This usually coincides with the start of the next school year. The accomplishment is a major event for the graduates. Graduation ceremonies are held in Arabic, English, and French, particularly in the private schools attended by wealthy families. At such graduations, cameras flash, parents dress in their finest, and students delight in passing

Long before they face the thanweyah a'mah, students take many tests, including midyear exams.

Al-Azhar University in Cairo is the second oldest university in the world, after University of Al Karaouine in Fez, Morocco. It is internationally known for its studies in Islam.

this life milestone.

For students who did well on the exam, admission to a college or university program is the next educational step. The government supports 13 major universities and 67 teacher colleges. Those who are accepted can attend tuition free. In the past 50 years, the number of women attending college has increased dramatically. Government programs that promote higher education for women have been successful. Today 56 percent of pharmacology students, 58 percent of dentistry students, and 45 percent of medical students are women. These studies lead to careers in high-paying, professional jobs.

Report Cards

When report cards come out, the students do not get As, Bs, or Cs. The results are exam scores: 43 out of 50, 36 out of 45, and so on. Every teacher rates students using a different scale. Parents need to know their math to determine if their children succeeded in class.

The modern and traditional meet in the sky as an apartment building and minarets tower above Cairo.

2 Everyday Life

THROUGHOUT EGYPT THERE IS LITTLE USE FOR AN ALARM CLOCK. AS DAWN BREAKS, muezzins issue the call to prayer from minarets, the high towers that are often found on mosques. Cairo has more than 1,000 minarets. But even the smallest village has a mosque—either with or without a minaret—and a muezzin who calls the faithful to prayer five times a day.

In addition to prayer, many teens' days are filled by school. For those who do not attend school, there is a need to earn money or help their families. The places that hire city teens are different from where rural teens work. City teens might take jobs in markets, restaurants, and garages. Rural teens, on the other hand, usually work before and after school helping their families with farming or fishing.

No matter where they live, the end of the day finds most Egyptian teens relaxing around the dinner table with their family.

muezzins
MOO-ehz-zins

Egypt
Population density
and political map

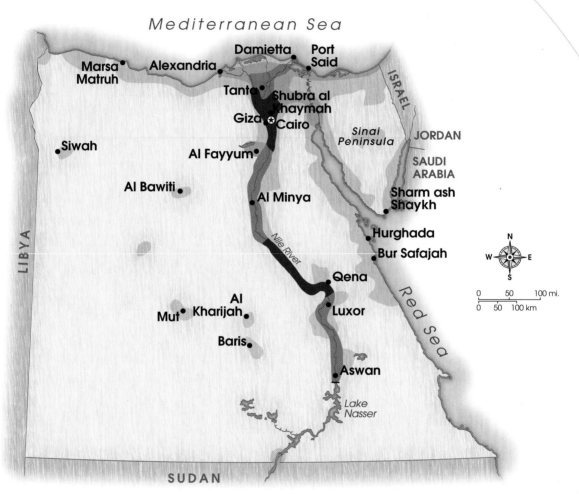

Mediterranean Sea

Marsa Matruh

Alexandria

Damietta

Port Said

ISRAEL

Tanta

Shubra al Khaymah

Giza

Cairo

Sinai Peninsula

JORDAN

SAUDI ARABIA

Siwah

Al Fayyum

Sharm ash Shaykh

Al Bawiti

Al Minya

Hurghada

Bur Safajah

LIBYA

Nile River

N
W E
S

0   50   100 mi.
0   50   100 km

Qena

Red Sea

Al Kharijah

Mut

Luxor

Baris

Aswan

Lake Nasser

SUDAN

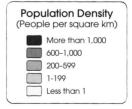

Population Density
(People per square km)

More than 1,000
600–1,000
200–599
1–199
Less than 1

City Life

Big city life for teens in Egypt is similar to big city life in most other countries. About half of Egypt's population lives in urban centers, but that percentage increases yearly. The largest cities are Alexandria, Aswan, and Greater Cairo, which is composed of Cairo, Giza, and Shubra al Khaymah. Together these cities form a primate city.

School is out by 1:30 P.M. Some teens stop by a coffeehouse or pick up a McArabia (a chicken sandwich served on flat bread), a popular offering at Egyptian McDonald's. Some teens head home to get started on homework or studying. Others join their teammates or friends to practice tennis, soccer, softball, or swimming.

These are children of middle-class or wealthy parents. They have opportunities that do not exist for teens of poor or rural families. Few teens from middle- or upper- income families have after-school jobs. If they do work, it is to help at home or in the family business.

Children in low-income families usually work to help their families survive. This work may take place in or out of the home. Girls may be asked to mind younger children, cook meals, do laundry, and clean house while their mothers work to earn money. If the family has a stall at a street market, teens may be expected to work there after school or instead of going to school. At age 14, young people can also get

City Driving

Egyptian city streets are filled with pedestrians, cyclists, and drivers. Cairo, for example, has more than 15 million people and 4 million cars. Teens get city-only drivers' licenses at age 16. Then at 18, they can get full drivers' licenses. Driving blends courage with healthy doses of horn blowing, especially since many Egyptian drivers ignore traffic signals and speed limits.

Many fishermen make their home in Cairo, where they can work in the Nile River.

regular jobs in factories, restaurants, or any place where adults might work. They are expected to do the same work as adults hired for the same job.

Rural Life

The people who till Egypt's soil are called the *fellahin*. As with city dwellers, rural Egyptians come from all income levels.

Wealthy and middle-income farmers fare well, but they only account for 6 percent of farms. The other 94 percent of farmers cultivate less than 5 *feddans* (5.2 acres, or 2 hectares) of land. For these farmers, the more children they have, the better the chance of

fellahin
feh-lah-HEEN

feddans
fehd-DANZ

getting work done.

Rural teens begin their days the same way as the rest of Egypt—to the call of the muezzin. Even without the call, they would get up at dawn. There is always stock to feed or other chores before school. After school, teens help plow, plant, and harvest. Farmers have an endless list of chores to do, and teens must do their share.

Because much of Egypt is dry, farmers depend on irrigation, mainly from the Nile, to water their crops.

In a family of fishermen, there is always work to do as well. Teens help by repairing nets, fixing the boat, handling the fish, and so on. The fishing industry is slowly modernizing. Today most fishing is done with trawlers and large nets hauled up by winches. In other areas, fishing may still mean a shallow boat, a hand-thrown net, and a small catch.

Rural girls usually work in the home. Traditionally, girls were often engaged to be married, and by 15 or 16 wedding plans were under way. By 18 most girls were already mothers. Today the trend of girls marrying young in Egypt's rural areas is changing. More girls are getting an education and making different life choices. They are looking to careers outside the home or planning to marry later in life. Nonetheless, most girls learn homemaking skills from an early age. They can cook, clean, and sew. During the teen years, a girl and her mother will sew beautiful linens for use when she is married.

Being Bedouin

The desert regions of the Sinai Peninsula are home to Bedouins, Egypt's nomadic ethnic group. Thoughts of Bedouins turn to camels, black goat-hair tents, and treks through the desert. Bedouins are desert dwellers, but today's tribes are turning in their camels for pickup trucks. Bedouins also have given up tents for housing settlements, medical clinics, and schools. They run hotels and restaurants at resorts like Dahab and send their sons to university.

Bedouin teens have more adult responsibilities than many of their urban contemporaries. However, many of their daily tasks are comparable to other

rural teens. A son might haul water for the family's goats or camels. His sister minds the younger children and helps with the cooking.

Teenage girls are considered adult women and wear black cloaks with colorful embroidery. Blue embroidery signifies a single woman, and red is for wives. Young men wear flowing white robes and turbans. Although this clothing may seem hot, it keeps the body cool in desert regions.

Often serving as guides, many Bedouins make their living in tourism.

The Aswan High Dam

Since the beginning of Egyptian history, the Nile River has affected all of Egypt. The Nile's floods carried new soil into the fields. Its water helped crops grow. Its fish fed the people. Its path was the primary transportation route in Egypt.

In 1960, Egypt began an effort that would change the lives of Egyptians forever. They began the massive engineering feat of damming the Nile River. After 10 years of building, the Aswan High Dam was completed. Lake Nasser, which was formed by the dam, lies along the Egypt-Sudan border. The lake is 313 miles (500 kilometers) across and provides water for agriculture throughout the year. Plans are under way to use some of Lake Nasser's water to create new farming villages along the Zayed Canal in the Sahara Desert.

The Nubians of the Nile

Another ethnic group in Egypt are the Nubians. They come from a narrow valley in Upper Egypt, near the Aswan Dam. This ethnic group is known for fishing and farming. For Nubians, life is forever linked to the Nile. As newborns, they are bathed in the river's chilly waters. When they marry, brides and grooms must wash—separately, of course—in the Nile. And widows wash away their sorrows in the life-giving waters.

The traditional Nubian lands currently lie under 200 feet (60 meters) of water. When the Aswan High Dam was completed, water filled the land and formed Lake Nasser. The government provided the Nubians with new homes and villages 370 miles (600 km) away from their homeland. However, the Nubians were not keen on the idea. They rebuilt their homes near the Nile and resumed their lives. For teen boys, that meant fishing or farming by their fathers' sides. Teen girls, like many girls in Egypt, were either working in their family home or already married.

Nubians are fun-loving, musical people. Every celebration is shared with the community and accompanied by the oud (a stringed instrument) and the *douff* (a drum). On special occasions, Nubian women wear colorful dresses

douff
dohf

Special Nubian celebrations include honoring the birthday of King Ramses, who ruled from 1270 to 1213 B.C.

with intricate beadwork and traditional white headscarves.

Food & Drink

City or country, Bedouin or Nubian, the breakfast of choice is *fuul,* cooked fava beans served with chopped hard-boiled egg and stuffed in a pita pocket. Lunch may be a repeat of breakfast fare. In the cities, *shwarma, kushari,* and falafel stands crowd street corners. Shwarma is thin slices

fuul
fool

shwarma
shuh-WAR-muh

kushari
KOO-sha-ree

33

of beef or lamb, slow-roasted over a fire, and layered onto long bread rolls. Kushari is a dish of lentils, rice, onions, and tomato sauce. A universal favorite is falafel. These deep-fried patties are made from crushed broad white beans that are spiced, flavored, and served in lettuce and pickle in a pita pocket.

Ai'ish, or bread, is the center of every meal, and serves as both a

ai'ish
ay-EESH

starch and a utensil. Most meals can be scooped up with wedges of bread. Peas, beans, chickpeas, and lentils are major ingredients for soups and stews. The prime protein source is lamb, which is stewed or grilled on skewers. Chicken and pigeon fill out the average family diet. In addition, Egyptians eat eggplant, tomatoes, onions, and peppers frequently because they grow well in the country.

Dinner might be kushari, a dish made with macaroni, lentils, and

Making Fuul

Making fuul takes planning—it is a two-day process. Broad fava beans are washed under cold water and then soaked for 24 hours. They are then rinsed again and placed in a casserole dish with twice as much water as beans. After the water is brought to a boil, the mixture is left to simmer for about 2 hours. Crushed

garlic, lemon juice, and olive oil are added to the mixture. The spices salt, paprika, and chopped parsley often complete the dish. Finally fuul is served with bread triangles, radishes, spring onions, and hard-boiled eggs. Egyptians of all ages enjoy this popular dish.

Because diners rely on their bread to scoop food up, utensils are rarely used in a traditional Egyptian meal.

tomatoes. The evening meal often includes pickles, yogurt, tahini (a sesame seed paste) or hummus (a chick-pea paste), and plenty of bread. If meat is served at dinner, it might be grilled, roasted, or minced buffalo, chicken, camel, or, of course, lamb. Grilled fish or fish soup are served every day in many homes. Many families share bowls of Molokhiya. This is a thick soup made with a spinachlike jute plant, garlic, and chicken, rabbit, or some other meat. Add bread, and dinner is complete.

Egyptians love sweets, and no dinner would be complete without baklava—a flaky pastry with nuts and honey. Another family favorite is *konafa*, thin strips of pastry served on a cream cheese base. Fruits are offered, depending on the season. Oranges, dates, pineapples, watermelons, guavas, mangoes, and pomegranates can be purchased whole or in liquid form from fruit and juice vendors in the city.

Shai and *ahwa*—tea and coffee—are drunk regularly throughout the country. Arabic coffee is served in coffeehouses on every corner and block of Cairo and Alexandria. The coffeehouse is the meeting place for men young and old. Men

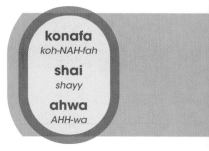

konafa
koh-NAH-fah

shai
shayy

ahwa
AHH-wa

Bread is Life

The Egyptian word for bread is ai'ish, which is also the word for "life." No meal is served without some type of bread. Pita bread, a flat pocket bread, is common. Bread serves as the common utensil for eating stews, soups, and salads. Rip off a portion of bread, scoop up some food, and enjoy!

play dominos, read the newspaper, and watch sports on TV. All the while they sip Arabic coffee—thick, strong, and gritty. Cups are small, holding barely five sips, and the coffee is sometimes flavored with cardamom, nutmeg, or cloves. In the heat of the summer, *karkade* slakes the thirst. Made from boiling

karkade
KAR-kah-day

hibiscus leaves, this drink is deep red in color and delicious.

In small villages, when evening comes, coffee cups are put aside. Street vendors park their carts for the night. The last call of the muezzin fills the air, as the devout unroll prayer rugs and offer thanks to God. In Cairo, the city never sleeps, particularly on weekends. Egyptians understand that life is a 24/7 event and take advantage of it.

Egyptian farmers grow enough fruits and vegetables to feed the country.

37

Public gardens in Egyptian cities give families a place to relax, eat, and play together.

3 The Importance of Family

AS EGYPT GROWS AND CHANGES, TRADITIONAL ATTITUDES ABOUT FAMILY ARE ALSO CHANGING. The traditional Egyptian family involves a close kin group: all the relatives in the father's line. A young married couple often lives near the husband's family or even with his parents. Living with her mother-in-law puts tremendous stress on a new bride. She must please not only her husband but his mother, too. The pressure is also on to produce a son and heir.

In cities, couples may not be able to live near the husband's parents. They must choose their homes by cost rather than location. The nuclear family—mom, dad, and the kids—is replacing the traditional-style family. This changes the relationships between children and their grandparents, aunts, uncles, and cousins. They do not see each other as often because they no longer live close to each other.

No matter where a family lives, Egyptian teens call their parents *Baba* and *Mama*, always with respect. Teens honor their elders. Respect is necessary when talking to

What's in a Name?
Common Egyptian names

Male Names

Name
Gamal
Hamza
Hassan or Hussein
Hosni
Ibrahim
Khaled
Mohammed
Youssef

Female Names

Name
Farah
Gamila
Hana
Hasnaa
Hosniya
Malak
Sahar

parents, older relatives, any adult, and even older brothers and sisters. Talking to her father, a teen would begin, "Most honored Baba," and go on from there.

Within a family, mothers are often addressed by nicknames. In the past this type of nickname would only be used after having a son. If a woman had five daughters and then a son Yousef, she would have been called Umm Yousef. Today it is becoming common for a woman to use her oldest child's name as part of her nickname. For example, the mother of a girl named Sahar is now called Umm (mother of) Sahar by family and friends.

Family values come from the strong moral structure of Islam. As a result, there is little street crime in Egypt. Heavy drinking or using drugs do not follow the prophet Muhammad's teachings, so crimes related to those practices are rare.

One of the most important aspects of family life is choosing a spouse. In the cities, young men and women have more of a say in whom they marry. A young man and woman might meet at work, share lunch, and get to know each other. If the man

Urban couples have more opportunities to spend time alone together than rural couples.

Following Muhammad

Members of the Muslim faith are followers of the prophet Muhammad, "The Praised One." Muhammad (570–632) believed that Allah, or God, spoke to him through the angel Gabriel. The ideas revealed through this contact were written in the Qur'an and are the basis for Islamic beliefs. The core beliefs of all Muslims are found in the Five Pillars of Islam. To be a good Muslim, a person must live according to these acts:

1. **The Testimony of Faith**—This is saying with conviction, *"La ilaha illa Allah, Muhammad rasool Allah."* This saying means "There is no true god but God, and Muhammad is the Messenger of God."

2. **Prayer**—A Muslim prays five times daily.

3. **Giving alms**—A Muslim gives to the needy.

4. **Fasting**—Muslims fast during the day for the entire month of Ramadan.

5. **Making the Hajj**—If financially able, every devout Muslim is expected to make a pilgrimage to Mecca in Saudi Arabia at least once during the Eid al-Adha holiday.

decides this is his chosen bride, he brings his family to meet her family. In rural districts, particularly in the far south (Upper Egypt), arranged marriages are common. Girls' parents frequently choose a cousin from the father's family

41

so that property will remain in the family's hands.

Women's Rights

For centuries, women in Egypt played a secondary role. The concept of women as equals or women having rights simply did not exist. Women depended totally on their fathers and their husbands for their survival. Women did not work outside the home and were believed to be less important than their husbands. A woman who only had daughters was called "mother of brides"—a serious insult. Within the family, males had value because they supported the family and carried on the family line. Sons stayed with their parents and cared for them in old age. Daughters went to their husbands' families.

In the past women were allowed to interact only with men who were related to them. They appeared fully veiled in public, and only a few—usually upper class women—were educated to read and write.

The Rights of Children

Children's rights have recently become a focal point in Egypt. In 1999, Egypt began the Children's Forum. This committee is formed from 1,000 child members selected from throughout Egypt. The forum gives children a chance to speak out about their concerns. Important issues include education, the college admission test, training for the future, and fair treatment for young women.

Traditionally, child rearing and child rights have fallen under the scope of parenting. The government agrees with this basic idea, but it has taken several issues under its wing. Parents can no longer marry off girls under 15 years of age. Government educational programs encourage parents to keep girls in school. The range of course offerings and number of universities have increased in the past 10 years. As a result, many more young women are pursuing professional studies and careers.

Women who work in agriculture often care for their children full time as well.

Marriage was traditionally by arrangement. A father would choose a suitable husband for his daughter. Although in theory she had the right to refuse, in practice it was very difficult to do so.

Even after the 1952 Egyptian Revolution, which increased the participation of women in public society, wives still could not easily get a divorce. Men could divorce their wives for any reason, while women had to go to court and were rarely successful if their husbands did not agree to the divorce. Divorced women retained custody of their sons only if they were younger than 12 and would get only one year of financial support.

In 1979, the Egyptian government passed the "women's rights law," which allowed women to divorce their husbands and keep custody of their children. Still, the divorce rate is low among Egyptians.

Laws have changed women's legal rights. However, the major factor that is changing views about women is the increase of women holding nonagricultural jobs. When women are able to support themselves with their own money, they have the freedom to make choices.

Egypt's first lady Suzanne Mubarak is at the forefront of change. In a speech

As women gain more education, their employment opportunities increase.

THE IMPORTANCE OF FAMILY

Illiteracy Over the Years

The gap between male and female illiteracy is steadily closing.

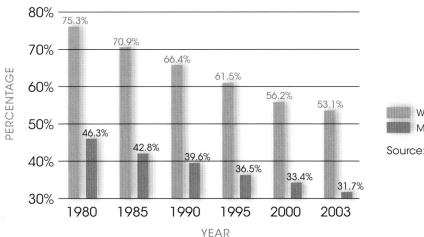

PERCENTAGE

| Women | 75.3% | 70.9% | 66.4% | 61.5% | 56.2% | 53.1% |
| Men | 46.3% | 42.8% | 39.6% | 36.5% | 33.4% | 31.7% |

YEAR: 1980 · 1985 · 1990 · 1995 · 2000 · 2003

Women
Men

Source: UN Common Database

Pioneer for Women

Hoda Sha'rawi pioneered women's rights in Egypt in the early 1900s. At the time an Egyptian's woman's place was in the kitchen. But Sha'rawi stood up for what she believed. She participated in Egypt's resistance against Great Britain's rule. She took part in establishing the Egyptian Women's Union in 1923. Sha'rawi founded two women's issue magazines, one in French and one in Arabic. Among Sha'rawi's major concerns were education for girls and legal rights for women.

given on International Woman's Day, Mubarak said:

"While following up all the exerted efforts, we feel proud and happy over the immense gains of the Egyptian woman. We have succeeded to make the community with all its segments come to discuss woman issues."

In recent years, Egyptian women have been elected to parliament and become government ministers, ambassadors, and judges.

Despite changing attitudes toward women, many Egyptian mothers struggle to survive. Many of them have husbands who work far from home. Others are in marriages where their husbands earn little money. And a rare few are divorced.

Mothers must still provide food and shelter for their children. Doing so is difficult without a well-paying job. More than half of adult women are illiterate, compared to about 32 percent of men. The lack of education means that the majority of Egyptian working women must work in low-paying jobs. They hold jobs as janitors, servants, hotel maids, and hospital aides.

Family Honor

One concern at the center of women's rights is the practice of female circumcision. Many Egyptians believe that a family's reputation is tied to the moral behavior of its women. They want to prevent teenage girls from having sex outside of marriage.

To ensure purity in women, many young girls are circumcised. The girl's outer genitals are cut off, and the vagina is sewn partially closed. The procedure is quite painful for the girl. The Egyptian government, Muslim clerics, and Coptic priests have spoken out strongly against the practice. In March 2005, Ahmend Talib, dean of the faculty of Sharia at the Al-Azhar University, said, "All practices of female circumcision and mutilation are crimes and have no relationship with Islam."

Despite these efforts, female circumcision continues to be practiced throughout the country. Parents who chose to have their daughters circumcised believe it will allow them to maintain family honor.

If women fail to live moral, pure lives in society's eyes, they can face serious consequences. In some areas of Egypt, male relatives kill women who have damaged the family's standing. These murders are called honor killings.

If a woman has sex before marriage, or if she marries a man her family does not approved of, the family's reputation suffers. If she is raped, that, too, shames the family, even though she is the victim. The idea behind honor killing is that by killing the woman, the family's honor is restored. This practice is not common, but it does happen every year in Egypt. (The number of annual killings has not been reported for more than a decade, so no one is sure how often it takes place.)

Changing Choices

Egypt teeters between two worlds: the traditional and the modern. The traditional world is Arabic and, for many, Muslim. In traditional Egypt, men did not consider women as equals. Traditional women did not try to change those beliefs. The modern world is Western and filled with technology. In modern Egypt, men must now compete with women in college. Men work with and for women in business and industry. That is an extreme turnaround in less than 100 years.

In years past, Egyptian men worked outside the home while the women worked inside the home. That was a fact of life. Today's teens face different work challenges and meet different opportunities. Because their elders have never faced these situations, teens cannot turn to their parents or grandparents for advice. Young Egyptians need to find a balance between the two worlds.

One area where this balance is obvious is in fashion. Egyptian women's fashions run the full range from Parisian designer garb to *hegab* that cover the body from head to toe. Women have a choice in what they wear. Today many teenage girls are choosing to cover their heads or veil their faces in the traditional way. This idea shocks their mothers, who believe that wearing the veil is a step backward in women's rights. Teens who wear the veil claim they are rejecting ideas of Western beauty.

hegab
hi-GAB

Many teen girls and young women prefer to cover their heads with scarves.

During Ramadan, Egyptians hang lamps of all types to light the streets.

4

Fasts, Feasts, & Fun

IT IS NOON ON A FRIDAY, AND MUSLIMS HEAD TO THE LOCAL MOSQUE. In the minaret, the muezzin calls the faithful to prayer. Below in the mosque, the men remove their shoes and take their places on the prayer rugs. The devout fall to their knees and bow their heads toward Mecca. This scene takes place in thousands of mosques throughout Egypt. Because Friday is the holy day for Muslims, work, schools, and public buildings are closed.

Roughly 90 percent of Egyptians are Muslims. Most are Sunnis, who are the largest sect of Islam, much like Protestants or Catholics are Christian. Muslims pray five times a day, although they are only required to do so at the mosque on Fridays. (Other times they may pray from home, school, or work.) In addition, Muslims celebrate several religious events spread out through the year. The events include fasts and feasts, and many focus on family.

The most important time of the year in Islam is Ramadan. Teens fast and pray during this monthlong holy time. As with all Islamic holidays, the date Ramadan begins depends on the Islamic calendar and changes every year.

Ramadan is the ninth month of the Islamic year. Muslims honor the time they believe God revealed the first portion of the Qur'an to the Prophet Muhammad. During Ramadan, Egyptian Muslims fast—they do not eat, drink, or smoke from sunrise to sunset. All Muslims except the very young, the sick, pregnant women and nursing mothers, and the elderly fast during Ramadan.

Teens take an active part in Ramadan, and schools are on short schedules during this month. As sunset comes, the family shares a meal called *iftar,* which means "breaking of the fast" or breakfast. Evenings are spent praying at the mosque, reading the Qur'an, and visiting with family and friends. Colorful lights shine on every city street. Egyptian Muslims look forward to this joyous festival.

iftar
IF-tahr

The Islamic Calendar

The Islamic calendar, also called the Hijri calendar, follows the moon. It contains 12 months of 29.53 days each, which adds up to 354.36 days per year. Because the Islamic year has 11 fewer days than the Gregorian calendar (the most widely used calendar in the world), the dates of holidays move forward on the Gregorian calendar every year. Religious holidays include Eid al-Adha, Ramadan, and Eid al-Fitr.

The Small Feast

Ramadan ends with Eid al-Fitr, the small feast. This is three days of feasting and a time when Egyptian children receive new clothes, toys, and money. The amount of money teens receive at Eid al-Fitr is generous. They can spend it on entertainment, clothes, books, or music. Muslims also use this occasion to fulfill one of the requirements of Islam: charity to the poor and needy.

Eid al-Adha, the Day of Sacrifice, comes after the traditional pilgrimages to Mecca in Saudi Arabia. Many Egyptians call this event Bayram al-Kabir. This holiday celebrates Abraham's willingness to sacrifice his

A carnival in Cairo provides teens with a fun place to spend the Eid al-Fitr holiday.

son to God. For this festival, a family sacrifices a lamb. The meat is doled out in thirds. One-third goes to the poor, one-third to neighbors, and one-third is eaten by the family. Again, this is a time when Muslims give their children gifts of money or toys. School is closed for the weeks when Eid al-Fitr and Eid al-Adha occur.

Coptic Holidays

About 10 percent of Egyptians are Christian. The majority follow the Coptic Christian faith. The most important holiday for Copts is Easter. As with Easter in other religions, the date changes from year to year. Coptic Easter falls on a Sunday between March 22 and April 25. Preceding Easter is the

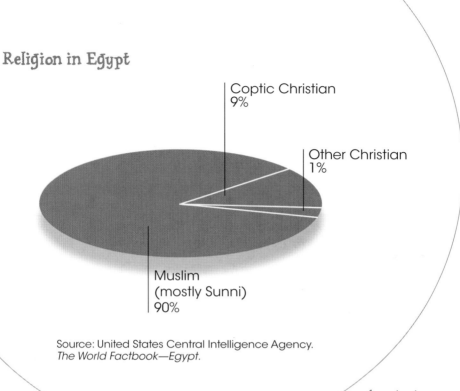

Religion in Egypt

Coptic Christian
9%

Other Christian
1%

Muslim
(mostly Sunni)
90%

Source: United States Central Intelligence Agency.
The World Factbook—Egypt.

season of Lent,
a time of fasting
and prayer. For religious Copts, fasting
means no meat, fish, eggs, cooking
oil, wine, or coffee during Lent, and
no eating between sunrise and sunset.
Fasting is a major element of the Coptic
religion, and fasting at some level takes
place 210 days of the year.

The Monday following Easter is
called Sham al-Nessim. It is a day for
family celebrations. The holiday's name
means "sniff the breeze." Egyptian
families head to parks, zoos, or even
the green medians between highways
for picnics.
Coptic Christmas
falls on January 7
each year. According to the
Coptic calendar, that was the date
of Christ's birth. In 2002, President
Hosni Mubarak declared January 7 a
national holiday for both Christians
and Muslims. This day is important to
Muslims because they consider Jesus to
be an important prophet. On Christmas
Eve, the Coptic Pope celebrates Mass
at 11 P.M. This service is shown on TV
throughout the country. Christmas in
Egypt comes complete with Christmas
trees, decorations, lights on the house,
and Santas galore.

Coptic Christians

When the Arabs conquered Egypt in 641, the majority of Egyptians followed the Christian faith. Today Christians, mainly Copts, are a religious minority in Egypt. They account for 6 million to 7 million Egyptians.

Copts attend a neighborhood church where they gather to worship, celebrate, and spend time with other Copts. The Copts sponsor many activities for Egyptian youth. Special youth classes held on Fridays provide religious education and social time.

Over the past 30 years, some Islamic extremist groups, such as al Gamaa al-Islamiyya (the Islamic Group) and al Ikhwan al-Muslimeen (the Muslim Brotherhood), have made Copts the targets of violence. Their crimes include burning churches, assaulting Copts in public, and kidnapping and murdering Copts. To escape this terrorism, many Copts have chosen to emigrate to Europe or North America.

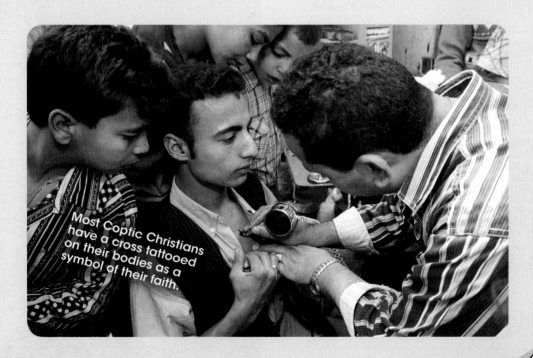

Most Coptic Christians have a cross tattooed on their bodies as a symbol of their faith.

Public Holidays

New Year's Day is the first public holiday of the Egyptian year. As in countries around the world, the day is celebrated with parties. Schools, businesses, and public buildings are closed for the holiday. Most hotels in the cities and resorts are booked up for New Year's Eve. Cruises on the Nile provide an elegant way to spend the evening and usually include a meal and a view of fireworks.

Three major national holidays deal with events in Egypt's history. June 18 celebrates the liberation of Egypt from British rule in 1922. The British sailed away from Port Said in northeastern Egypt. Many Egyptians call this holiday Liberation Day or Evacuation Day. It also celebrates the day that Egypt was declared a republic. Flags fly high on Liberation Day throughout Egypt.

July 23 honors the 1952 revolution that overthrew the rule of King Farouk. A group of young army officers began a military attack to end the monarchy

Egypt's Public Holidays

New Year's Day	January 1
Coptic Christmas	January 7
Labor Day	May 1
Liberation Day	June 18
Revolution Day	July 23
Armed Forces Day	October 6

in Egypt. Once the officers were in action, they decided to start a republic. One of the officers who started the movement was Gamal Abdel Nasser. He later became president of Egypt. On Revolution Day, schools and businesses are closed and parades honor the military.

Armed Forces Day comes on October 6. It remembers October 6, 1973, when Egyptian troops crossed the Suez Canal during a war with Israel. Egyptian warplanes flew over the Suez and attacked an Israeli military center. The Egyptians called this attack Operation Badr.

In honor of the new millennium in 2000, fireworks lit the sky over the pyramids of Giza.

Here Comes the Bride

Getting married is important to Egyptians. The family is the center of Egyptian society, and marriage holds the family together. As with school and family life, dating and marriage are different in the cities and in rural areas.

City life offers many opportunities for young men and women to meet and spend time together. Most teens go out in groups. A group of girls can easily meet a group of boys at a sporting event, at the university, or in the hundreds of nightclubs that cater to young people.

Today's engagements are long. A home needs to be planned, and collecting the money to pay for and furnish a home is expensive. The average Egyptian income is about 150 Egyptian pounds (U.S.$44) per month, and the average cost of a marriage in Egyptian cities is 100,000 Egyptian pounds (U.S.$30,000).

Engagement and marriage in the rural areas, particularly in Upper Egypt, is quite different. There is no dating, because there is no place for boys and girls to meet. The two most common ways to find a bride are through a matchmaker and by picking a cousin. Cousins marrying each other remains a widespread practice among Upper Egyptian cultures. Although the law requires that a girl be at least 16 before marrying, young girls may become engaged long before they are teenagers.

A rural wedding is a community event covering three or more days.

Modern urban weddings have Western influences, such as a white dress for the bride.

The henna patterns are very detailed and elaborate.

Times are changing for brides in Egypt. Fifty years ago girls would go directly into an arranged marriage. Education has forced a dramatic change. Now girls want to finish school and choose their own husbands. They want to be involved in the decisions that affect their lives.

Henna Night

For the bride and her female friends, henna night is a highlight of the busy time. The bride is honored with gifts, much like at a bridal shower. Her hands and legs are painted with henna, a reddish-brown dye. Although this is a temporary tattoo, it will remain for several weeks.

Henna night has become a fad that has swept from Upper Egypt into Cairo. In modern henna parties, pop music blares over the voices of chatting women. Snacks and sodas are served. Since many urban women find wearing henna to work for several weeks inappropriate, the one thing missing from urban henna nights is henna!

On one night, the bride's female family and friends gather and decorate her hands and feet with henna designs. A party for the groom includes the guests and the men of both families. A separate event is held for the bride with singing and dancing. The bride's family makes a great fuss of moving the bride's wedding goods, such as linens and furniture, to the new home. The groom may present the bride with a dowry of cash and gold and silver jewelry. The bride and groom do not spend any time together until the marriage is official.

Though the legal age of employment is 14, about 2.7 million younger children are working full time.

5

Working Hard for a Living

MAHMOUD HAS HELD A JOB AT A SMALL ALEXANDRIA RESTAURANT FOR TWO YEARS. The 14-year-old washes dishes, cuts vegetables, mops the floors, and buses the tables. The boy works six days a week, from 10 A.M. until nearly midnight. Ever since Mahmoud finished primary school, he has worked to help feed his family.

This young man is one of Egypt's 2.7 million child workers between the ages of 6 and 14. These children have limited schooling. They are caught in a spider's web of poverty. Some child workers live with both of their parents. Some have only one parent. These children have no choice but to work.

In Egypt, one in five people lives below the poverty line. The upper 10 percent of the population purchases 25 percent of all consumer goods. Millions more live a hand-to-mouth existence. They struggle to get enough money for food and clothing. Often, to help support his family, a husband must look for work far away. The fathers leave rural Egypt for jobs in Cairo or Alexandria. Some go to Libya or the Persian Gulf to find work. To help out with money, children must also work.

Generally, city children work in restaurants, laundries, and textile mills. Rural children work at farming or fishing. Depending on the area, children make up between 25 percent and 60 percent of the workforce in Egypt's cotton fields.

Government leaders worry about child labor. Children who must work to eat never get enough education to get better paying jobs. They become locked in the cycle of poverty. Laws control the

Egypt is the world's top producer of long-fibered cotton, which is known for its durability.

A wide variety of items are sold in the souq, ranging from food to perfume to clothing.

amount of time children can work and have improved the conditions under which they work. However, passing laws is one thing; enforcing them is another. As UNICEF's Senior Program Officer Hannan Suleiman says:

"As things stand, there's little doubt that many poor families have no alternative but to take their children out of school and put them to work, simply in order to make ends meet."

Many children work either full time or part time in the *souq*, open-air markets. Merchants need additional workers, so they have their children work for them. Some children spend the entire day

souq
sook

Young children sell bread from the trays they balance on the top of their heads.

in the market. Others only work after school. Whether selling fuul or fruit juice from a cart or spices in the Khan al-Khalili street market in Cairo, these children must work hard. They also have a future. Most stalls are passed down from father to son. Plus these children have homes, families, and friends. Not all children are so lucky.

Street Kids

Between 600,000 and 1 million Egyptian children either live on city streets or are forced to work full time outdoors. Some of these children are as young as 6 or 7 and survive by begging. How could this happen?

If a mother cannot feed all her children, the older ones are forced to leave home and fend for themselves. These children, referred to as street kids, live harsh lives. They wander around at night, afraid to sleep because it is too dangerous. They travel in packs like wolves, begging money from tourists. They do small jobs and demand baksheesh, or small tips. For many Egyptian workers, this small amount is what makes it possible to eat daily. Baksheesh is expected for every service. Delivering a paper, parking a car, waiting on tables, and even keeping shoes at mosques are worthy of a tip. Teens

working on the street depend on baksheesh to buy food and clothing.

Conflicts between the police and street teens have become a serious problem. Anwar, a 15-year-old street kid, said:

"I was in the Giza police station for a week before they sent me to al Azbekiya [the youth facility]. At the Giza station I was with thieves who hit us and made us sit in the bathroom. ... There were adults and kids. The smallest kid was nine."

There are few solutions for the problems that street kids face every

Earning Potential

Salaries in Egypt seem quite low compared to equivalent jobs in Western nations. For example, a teacher may earn only 200 Egyptian pounds (about U.S.$35) a month. A beginning engineer might take home 300

Egyptian pounds (U.S.$53) a month, while the starting salary for police officers would be between 50 and 75 Egyptian pounds (U.S.$9–$13). However, the cost of living is also much lower. Money does go further in Egypt than it would in many other places.

day. Their lives bear little in common with the children of middle income or wealthy families.

Hope for the Future

The government has developed a broad program to help Egypt's teens succeed in the workplace. The government knows that today's youth form the spine of Egypt's economy in the future. Special programs help young men and women learn trades and develop skills. They can apply what they have learned in agriculture, petroleum-related jobs, the textile industry, and computer science.

Farming is a major industry in Egypt. Thirty-two percent of employed Egyptians work in agriculture. And nearly 15 percent of the gross domestic product comes from agriculture. Teens in farming families are expected to do their share of chores. They help produce and harvest many of Egypt's major agricultural products: cotton, rice, corn, wheat, beans, fruit, and vegetables. Cattle and livestock are limited, but some wealthy farmers have herds of cattle, water buffalo, sheep, and goats.

Nearly 46,000 young men have received farmland from the government. The government is providing utilities,

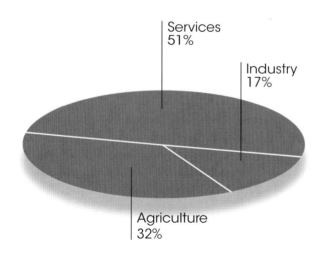

Division of Labor

Services
51%

Industry
17%

Agriculture
32%

Source: United States Central Intelligence Agency.
The World Factbook—Egypt.

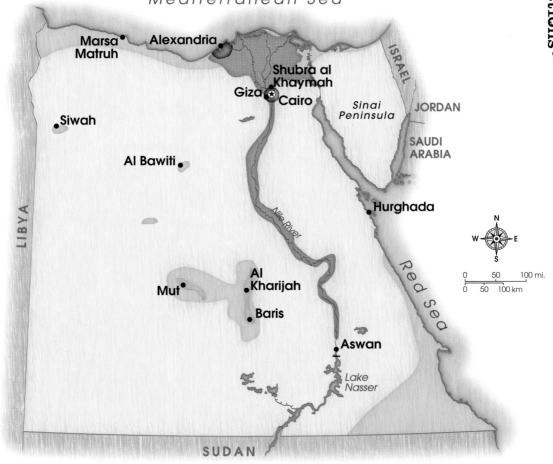

Egypt
Land use map

Mediterranean Sea

Marsa Matruh
Alexandria
Shubra al Khaymah
Giza Cairo
Siwah
Sinai Peninsula
Al Bawiti
Hurghada
Al Kharijah
Mut
Baris
Aswan
Lake Nasser

LIBYA
ISRAEL
JORDAN
SAUDI ARABIA
Red Sea
Nile River
SUDAN

N
W   E
S

0   50   100 mi.
0   50   100 km

Land Use

- Irrigated cropland
- Grazing/ nomadic herding
- Manufacturing
- Oasis
- Unproductive land

roads, and other support for the farms. Agricultural workers are in high demand because Egypt needs to feed its growing population. The population is increasing at a rate of 1.75 percent per year. That is greater than the rates of booming countries such as India (1.38 percent) or China (0.59 percent).

Government officials recognize that this population growth will affect other areas in their country. They are working to address these needs. In 2002, for instance, the government generated more than 550,000 new jobs. These jobs included doctors, teachers, and social workers in the cities.

Egypt is undergoing a major economic surge. The country houses 75 industrial zones with 20,000 factories. And three new factories are set up daily. These factories provide work in textiles, chemical processing, food processing, construction, and oil-based industries. Tourism provides service industry jobs for guides, restaurant workers, cab drivers, entertainers, and a host of other seasonal workers.

One area in which young men and women can get education and training while also being paid is the

Teens can earn a little money selling maps or items such as head coverings to tourists.

Military police on camelback serve as guards at the pyramids and other national treasures.

military. Egypt has five academies dedicated to military training: the Military Academy (army), the Naval Academy, the Air Force Academy, the Military Technical Academy, and the Air Defense Academy. The education is free, and space is limited. As a result, secondary school graduates face stiff competition for a spot. All candidates must have above-average exam scores. Candidates for the Military Technical Academy need high scores in math and science. Students who succeed in the Egyptian military receive both a quality education and a guaranteed job afterward.

Though traditional coffee shops are filled mainly with men, women often gather at modernized versions.

6

Finding Time for Fun

FLUSH WITH CASH AFTER EID AL-FITR, MANY URBAN TEENS HEAD TO THE MALL.

The First Residence Mall in Giza has fabulous stores like those in Paris, Rome, London, Tokyo, or New York. Shopping is a common pastime among Egyptian teens, especially among upper-income families. This might mean heading to modern high-rise malls or to the souq. In the Khan al-Khalili souq, Egyptian women sort through gold bracelets and multicolored beads. Fabric stalls offer lengths of excellent Egyptian cotton.

Men prefer to relax with other men, often in traditional coffee shops. They play games of taula (backgammon) or talk politics or business. They discuss how a favorite team is doing in the latest tournament. They read the paper over small cups of strong coffee. Teenage boys join their fathers in this scene. Coffee shops attract men from all economic groups. When a man of any age has free time and a few coins in his pocket, he heads to his local coffee shop.

taula
TOW-lah

Playing Taula

In traditional coffee shops throughout Cairo, men meet in serious combat over a game of taula. They shake and role the dice. They move their counters. Hands fly across the board, shifting black or white markers from one triangle to the next. Toward the end of the game, the speed slows and strategy takes over.

One player reaches 31—the winning score. His opponent grits his teeth over the loss. Perhaps tomorrow …

Taula, or backgammon, is played on a board with 24 triangles in four pockets. Players take turns moving according to the numbers on the dice. The goal is to move the 15 counters from the home-base triangle to the opponent's home base and score. Teenage boys learn the game from their fathers and grandfathers.

Taula is popular with Bedouin children.

For teens, weekends can be especially fun. Some teens just hang out with friends—girls with girlfriends, boys with other boys. Or the groups may venture out for some fun. There are hundreds of local clubs, sports venues, movie theaters, shopping malls, and parks that welcome teens. Curfew for 17- and 18-year-olds is usually midnight on weekends. Special arrangements to stay out later are common when teens attend a concert or sports event. For working teens, the weekend brings a day off to spend time with family or friends. Fun can be a pickup *futbol* (soccer) game or listening to music on the radio.

futbol
FUHT-bol

Sports for Everyone

Sports attract young and old, boys and girls. According to Fareeda, a girl in

The pyramids of Giza provide a backdrop for an informal game of futbol.

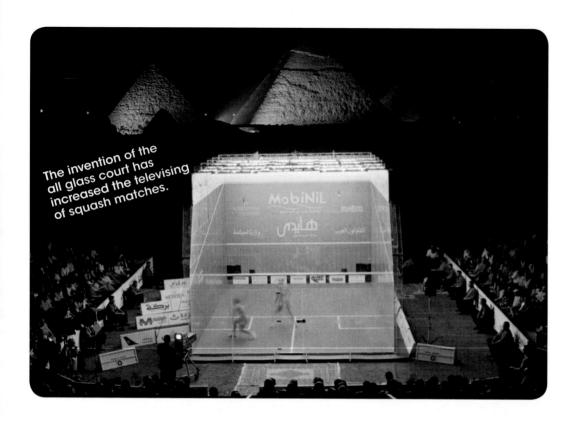

The invention of the all glass court has increased the televising of squash matches.

secondary school:

"After school, if you play any sports in a sports club—you might have practice. My favorite sport is basketball and I have practice every other day."

Egypt is mad about futbol, particularly since the Egyptian team won the 2006 Africa Cup. Whenever a match is telecast, the coffeehouses fill up with avid fans, who cheer every goal and groan over missed shots.

Futbol can be played anywhere there is open space and a ball. It is popular among people from all income levels. As for organized matches, Egypt has national, league, and local teams. A pickup game in a local park is as exciting to the players as a national "friendly" match in Cairo's futbol stadium.

Squash, an indoor racquet game, has a large following. In fact, it is President Mubarak's favorite game. Each year, *Al-Ahram*, a newspaper in Cairo sponsors an international squash tournament. World-class players compete in glass courts set up beside the Great Pyramids in Giza.

Motor sports attract a sizable Egyptian audience. The most popular is the Cairo Derby, a road race that today features four-wheel drive vehicles and trail bikes. More than 100 years old, this race once pitted teams of camel drivers against each other. According to Omar, a teenage fan, "The Cairo derby between Al Ahly and El Zamalek is one of the most anticipated events in Egypt as both teams are bitter rivals ever since the start of the nineteenth century."

Wealthy and poor alike line the route to cheer for their favorites during the race.

Culture & Arts

Egypt's teens grow up surrounded by a long and ancient heritage. In Giza, they live in apartments that back up to the Great Pyramids. In Alexandria, a modern-day library recalls the extensive collection of the former Great Library,

Teens can easily learn about their heritage at one of Egypt's many museums, such as the Egyptian Museum in Cairo.

built more than 2,000 years ago. Every major Egyptian city has a museum dedicated to ancient times.

Egypt also has a strong sense of the present and dreams for its future. This awareness is seen in the country's literature. The most famous authors include the 1988 Nobel Prize-winning Naguib Mahfouz. His novels and short stories shaped the nation's literature. Mahfouz's style resembles ancient storytelling, similar to the parables found in the Qur'an.

In the world of dance, Egypt offers a fairly unique dance form: belly dancing. Belly dancing classes offer women of all ages an opportunity to learn this skill. With swiveling hips and gyrating bellies, belly dancers are a staple of nearly every Egyptian movie. Belly dancing stars such as Tahiyya Carioca and Fifi Abdou draw huge audiences. Their paychecks reach as much as $10,000 per performance.

Belly dancers often perform on cruise ships and other public venues.

Lights! Camera! Action!

For decades, Egypt has been the movie capital of the Arab world. Egyptian studios produce 60 to 70 projects a year. Of those, 15 to 20 are feature films, and the rest are television programs. Egypt's major cities have movie theaters—cinemas—that show both Arabic and English movies. Tickets cost 10–20 Egyptian pounds (U.S. $1.80–$3.60), and most theaters are modern multiplex operations.

Egypt's most famous movie maker is Yousef Chahine, who has directed a number of award-winning movies. His most recent movies include *Alexandria … New York* and *Silence … We're Filming*. Chahine's *Al Mohager* features popular star Youssra in the feature role, bringing her skills as a belly dancer to the silver screen. Egypt's Omar Sharif appears in both Egyptian and internationally made movies.

Among the rising young stars, singer Tamer Hosny and the talented Nelly Karim have huge fan clubs. Karim works as a movie and television actress and a model, and is an accomplished ballerina.

Action movies are popular in Egypt.

Coffee shop televisions are most often tuned in to sports.

Media & Music

Egypt's media falls under close government scrutiny. Most news outlets are either government-owned or have a semi-official focus. A semi-official newspaper reports news in a way that is approved by the government. Most of the nation's newspapers are published in Alexandria or Cairo. Some, such as *Al-Ahram* and *Egyptian Gazette*, have countrywide distribution. Dozens of Egyptian papers and magazines now appear on the Internet in English, French, and Arabic.

Television and radio stations are also government controlled. There are 98 television broadcast stations, 42 AM radio stations, and 14 FM stations, most owned and operated by the government. News comes in Arabic, French, and English. Viewers can also watch satellite feeds of CNN and BBC World.

Teens prefer watching MTV, *Camera Khafeya* (the Egyptian version of *Candid Camera*), and the *Simpsons* dubbed in Arabic. Cartoon versions of futbol series, *Captain Majid* and *Captain Rami*, draw audiences from young children through grandparents. Anime shows are popular with teens in Egypt. *Art Teenz*, *MBC3*, and *Spacetoon E* have plenty of fans tuned in each week.

Television channels promoting music pop up regularly. Popular channels—Rotana, Rotana Tarab, Mazzika, Melody Arabia, MC, Zoom, and ART Music—feature new singers from Egypt, Europe, and the United States. Teens rave over pop idols Amr Diab and Tamer Hosny, who are played throughout the Arab world.

Teens also listen to Umm Kulsoum, a singer who made her first recording in 1926. During her nearly 50-year career, Kulsoum recorded more than 300 songs. Although she died in 1975, her music is still played over the radio and is popular with all ages.

Teens often go to clubs to listen to live music. The range of music covers everything from pop to rap, Arabic to European. Egyptian singers understand that they must choose their music carefully. There can be no swearing, violence, or vulgar suggestions in any songs. Gangsta rap is definitely "out" for Egyptian teen bands.

Teen bands generally sing English rock covers mixed with original songs. They play on guitars, drums, and

Wust el Balad, or Downtown, is a popular live band in Cairo. Their music is a mix of Arabic music, jazz, blues, and Latin.

Pop Idols

Tamer Hosny (1977-)

Tamer Hosny is the new generation of Egyptian musician. Multitalented Hosny is a singer, actor, and composer. He also has a passion for soccer and opera. His single "Arrab Habibi" was played heavily on satellite music stations.

Amr Diab (1961-)

Amr Diab is one of the most famous pop singers in Egypt. His first album *Ya Taree* attracted great attention in the Arab world when it debuted in 1983. He is known for an innovative music form called Mediterranean Music. This music blends Western and Middle Eastern rhythms. Diab has been considered the best singer in the Arab world since the early 1990s.

Tamer Hosny

stringed instruments. Some pop musicians find that traditional Egyptian instruments—the oud and the douff—just do not work when making modern music.

On the Road

For those who can afford it, vacation time is a break from the heat of Cairo or Giza. Egyptian families head to the beach or to an oasis to escape the heat and crowds of Egypt's cities.

The beaches on the Mediterranean Sea have been popular for many years. Today, however, Egyptians head for the Red Sea resorts of Sharm el-Sheikh or

Hurghada. Egyptians enjoy the white sand beaches and the deep turquoise water. Teens eat breakfast with their parents, but they often do not see them again until late at night. They browse through the shops on the boardwalk or go parasailing. Many teens snorkel or scuba dive, rent sailboats, or just sun themselves.

For those who like sand, but do not care for the beach, there are many oases that offer peace, quiet, and clean air.

The number of resorts in Sharm el-Sheikh increased from three in 1982 to 91 in 2000.

79

Egypt
Topographical map

Mediterranean Sea

As Sallum
Marsa Matruh
Alexandria
Nile Delta
Damietta
ISRAEL
Suez Canal
Ismailiyah
Suez
Giza
Fayoum Oasis
Cairo
Qattara Depression
Siwah Oasis
Siwah
Sinai Peninsula
JORDAN
Mount Catherine
SAUDI ARABIA
Lake Qarun
Baharia Oasis
Sharm ash Shaykh
Farafirah Oasis
Nile River
Eastern Desert
Hurghada
LIBYA
Western Desert
S A H A R A
Dakhilah Oasis
Nile Valley
Red Sea
Al Kharijah
Kharijah Oasis
Red Sea Hills
Aswan Dam
Aswan
Lake Nasser
Zayed Canal
SUDAN

N
W   E
S

0   50   100 mi.
0   50   100 km

Major railroad

Only 60 miles (100 km) from Cairo lies the Fayoum Oasis. Fayoum mixes historic temples, archaeological digs, greenery, and the stunningly beautiful Lake Qarun. Teens enjoy rowing on the water and hiking through the temples dedicated to Sobek, the ancient crocodile god. Vacations are brief, and within a few days, it is back to the city and school for most teens.

Hot Spots

While native Egyptians may head to the resorts to relax, tourists are more likely to head to some of the ancient treasures. The most famous tourist attractions are the Giza pyramids and the Great Sphinx.

The pyramids of Giza have stood for about 4,500 years. Built as tombs for kings, they were filled with treasures. Today many of the valuable items are on display in museums.

The Great Sphinx was built around the same time as the pyramids. The ancient Egyptians built the statue by carving the head and body out of a giant piece of limestone. They then cut stone blocks to make legs and paws.

Looking Ahead

MOST PEOPLE CANNOT IMAGINE BUILDINGS THAT HAVE BEEN AROUND FOR THOUSANDS OF YEARS. They cannot imagine living within touching distance of pyramids, sphinxes, and statues of ancient gods. Egyptian teens live among these wonders, but they look beyond the past toward the future. They live in today's world. School rules the lives of many teens. When not studying, teens enjoy the same things as other teens from around the world: music, sports, movies, and shopping. But some differences do exist.

Religion is very important to Egyptian teens. Many believe in the teachings of Islam and meet the demands of the prophet Muhammad. Prayer comes five times daily, and faithful Muslims avoid swearing, alcohol, and drugs. Part of Muslim life is to value family and show respect for elders.

Today's modern Egyptian teens go out with their friends to movies and clubs. They talk endlessly to friends on their cell phones. They listen to music that probably drives their parents crazy. They are, in every sense, teenagers; their hopes and dreams are just like every other teen's. They want friends, a family, freedom within limits, and a bright future.

83

At a Glance

Official name: Arab Republic of Egypt

Capital: Cairo

People

Population: 78,887,007

Population by age group:
0–14 years: 32.6%
15–64 years: 62.9%
65 years and older: 4.5%

Life expectancy at birth: 71.29 years

Official language: Arabic

Other common languages: English and French

Religions:
Muslim: 90%
Coptic: 9%
Other Christian: 1%

Legal ages
Alcohol consumption: 21
Driver's license: 16 (city-only), 18 (full license)
Employment: 14
Marriage: 16 (females), 18 (males)
Military service: 18
Voting: 18

Government

Type of government: Republic

Chief of state: President, elected by popular vote for six-year term

Head of government: President

Lawmaking body: Majlis al-Sha'b (People's Assembly) and Majlis al-Shura (Advisory Council); members are either elected by popular vote or appointed by the president

Administrative divisions: 26 *muhafazat* (governorates)

Independence: February 28, 1922 (from the United Kingdom)

National symbols:
Bird: Saladin's eagle
Flower: Egyptian lotus
Landmark: Great Sphinx of Giza

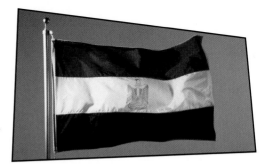

Geography

Total Area: 400,580 square miles (1,001,450 square kilometers)

Climate: Desert; hot, dry summers, moderate winters

Highest point: Mount Catherine, 8,676 feet (2,629 meters)

Lowest point: Qattara Depression, 439 feet (133 m) below sea level

Major river: Nile

Major landform: Libyan Desert

Economy

Currency: Egyptian pound

Population below poverty line: 20%

Major natural resources: petroleum, natural gas, iron ore, phosphates, manganese, limestone, gypsum, talc, asbestos, lead, zinc

Major agricultural products: cotton, rice, corn, wheat, beans, fruits, vegetables, cattle, water buffalo, sheep, goats

Major exports: crude oil and petroleum products, cotton, textiles, metal products, chemicals

Major imports: machinery, equipment, foodstuffs, chemicals, wood products, fuels

Historical Timeline

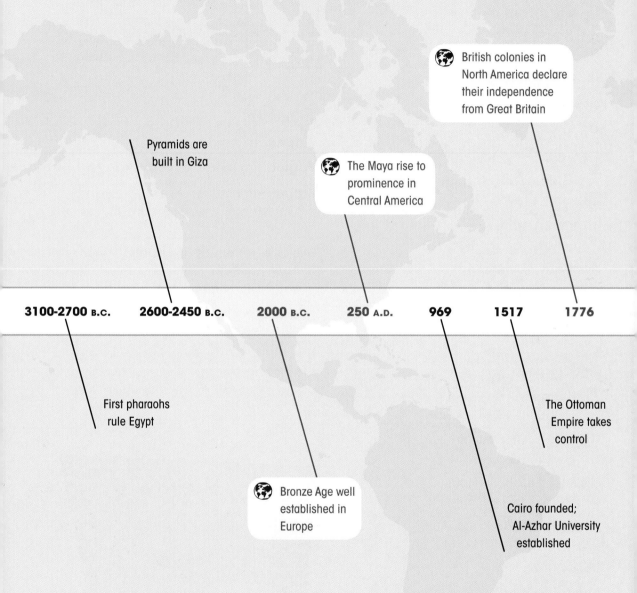

British colonies in North America declare their independence from Great Britain

Pyramids are built in Giza

The Maya rise to prominence in Central America

3100-2700 B.C.   **2600-2450** B.C.   **2000** B.C.   **250** A.D.   **969**   **1517**   **1776**

First pharaohs rule Egypt

The Ottoman Empire takes control

Bronze Age well established in Europe

Cairo founded; Al-Azhar University established

Historical World Event

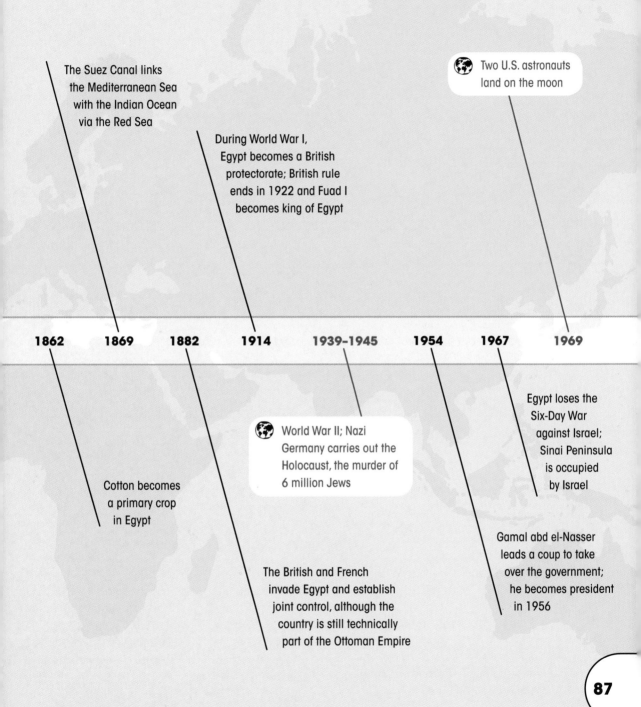

The Suez Canal links
the Mediterranean Sea
with the Indian Ocean
via the Red Sea

During World War I,
Egypt becomes a British
protectorate; British rule
ends in 1922 and Fuad I
becomes king of Egypt

🌐 Two U.S. astronauts
land on the moon

| 1862 | 1869 | 1882 | 1914 | 1939–1945 | 1954 | 1967 | 1969 |

Egypt loses the
Six-Day War
against Israel;
Sinai Peninsula
is occupied
by Israel

🌐 World War II; Nazi
Germany carries out the
Holocaust, the murder of
6 million Jews

Cotton becomes
a primary crop
in Egypt

Gamal abd el-Nasser
leads a coup to take
over the government;
he becomes president
in 1956

The British and French
invade Egypt and establish
joint control, although the
country is still technically
part of the Ottoman Empire

87

Historical Timeline

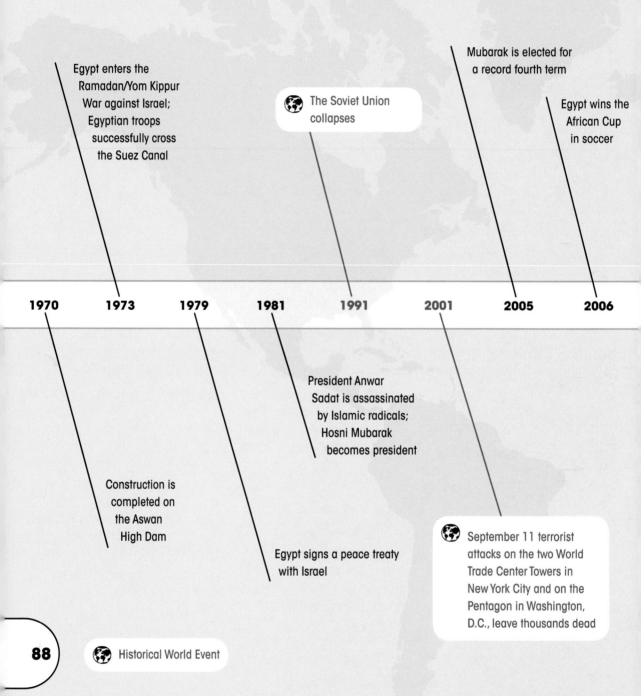

Egypt enters the Ramadan/Yom Kippur War against Israel; Egyptian troops successfully cross the Suez Canal

Mubarak is elected for a record fourth term

The Soviet Union collapses

Egypt wins the African Cup in soccer

1970   1973   1979   1981   1991   2001   2005   2006

President Anwar Sadat is assassinated by Islamic radicals; Hosni Mubarak becomes president

Construction is completed on the Aswan High Dam

Egypt signs a peace treaty with Israel

September 11 terrorist attacks on the two World Trade Center Towers in New York City and on the Pentagon in Washington, D.C., leave thousands dead

Historical World Event

Glossary

circumcision	surgical removal of part of the reproductive organs; in males, the foreskin of the penis is removed, and in females, part or all of the clitoris is removed
gross domestic product	the total value of all goods and services produced in a country during a specific period
Islam	religion founded on the Arabian Peninsula in the seventh century by the prophet Muhammad
liberation	the act of freeing a person, group, or nation
monarchy	a type of government in which a king or queen is the head of state
mosque	the Islamic place of worship
muezzins	men who call the faithful to prayer at an Islamic mosque
Muslim	a religious follower of Islam, or referring to a follower of Islam
piastres	the coinage of Egypt
primate city	city that is at least twice as populated as the second largest city in a country; serves as the cultural, economic, and often political center of the nation
technical	having to do with machines or computers
trawlers	fishing boats designed to drag a fishing net along the bottom of the sea
vocational	referring to a particular field of employment, usually a field that requires skilled workers such as mechanics, plumbers, or carpenters

Additional Resources

IN THE LIBRARY

Fiction and nonfiction titles to further enhance your introduction to teens in Egypt, past and present.

Gregory, Kristiana. *Cleopatra VII: Daughter of the Nile*. New York: Scholastic, 1999.

Levitin, Sonia. *Escape from Egypt*. New York: Puffin Books, 1996.

Barghusen, Joan D. *Daily Life in Ancient and Modern Cairo*. Minneapolis: Runestone Press, 2000.

Cox, Vicki. *Hosni Mubarak*. Philadelphia: Chelsea House Publishers, 2003.

Kheirabadi, Masoud. *Islam*. Philadelphia: Chelsea House Publishers, 2004.

Perl, Lila. *The Ancient Egyptians*. New York: Franklin Watts, 2004.

Wilson, Neil. *Egypt*. Chicago: Raintree Steck-Vaughn Publishers, 2001.

Zuehlke, Jeffrey. *Egypt in Pictures*. Minneapolis: Lerner, 2002.

ON THE WEB

For more information on this topic, use FactHound.
1. Go to www.facthound.com
2. Type in this book ID: 0756532949
3. Click on the Fetch It button.

Look for more Global Connections books.

Teens in Australia	*Teens in Iran*	*Teens in Saudi Arabia*
Teens in Brazil	*Teens in Israel*	*Teens in South Korea*
Teens in Canada	*Teens in Japan*	*Teens in Spain*
Teens in China	*Teens in Kenya*	*Teens in Venezuela*
Teens in England	*Teens in Mexico*	*Teens in Vietnam*
Teens in France	*Teens in Nigeria*	
Teens in India	*Teens in Russia*	

Source Notes

Page 46, column 1, line 3: Suzanne Mubarak. "Woman Issues Basic Component in State's Plans for Comprehensive Development." Egypt State Information Service. 14 March 2007. www.sis.gov.eg/En/Women/Wday/100800000000000002.htm

Page 46, column 2, line 10: Eunice Menka. "Islam Does Not Support Female Circumcision – Expert." GhanaHomePage. 16 March 2005. 14 March 2007. www.ghanaweb.com/GhanaHomePage/NewsArchive/artikel.php?ID=77396

Page 61, column 1, line 7: Simon Ingram. "Reclaiming Childhood: UNICEF and Partners Protect Child Labourers in Egypt." UNICEF. 11 April 2006. 14 March 2007. www.unicef.org/infobycountry/egypt_33288.html

Page 63, column 2, line 7: "Voices of Egypt's Street Children." Human Rights Watch. 2006. 14 March 2007. www.hrw.org/press/2003/02/egypt-test021903.htm

Page 72, column 1, line 2: "Your Egypt." BBC World Service. 14 March 2007. www.bbc.co.uk/worldservice/learningenglish/radio/specials/1214_le_world/page52.shtml

Page 73, column 1, line 6: Ibid.

Pages 84–85, At a Glance: United States. Central Intelligence Agency. *The World Factbook—Egypt.* 8 March 2007. 14 March 2007. www.cia.gov/library/publications/the-world-factbook/geos/eg.html

Select Bibliography

Al-Ahram Weekly On-line. 14 March 2007. www.ahram.org.eg/weekly/

Amim, Galal. *Whatever Happened to the Egyptians?* New York: The American University in Cairo Press, 2000.

Bayat, Asef. "Cairo's Poor: Dilemmas of Survival and Solidarity." *Middle East Report* 202 (Winter 1996). 14 March 2007. www.merip.org/mer/mer202/poor.html

Beattie, Andrew. *Cairo: A Cultural History.* New York: Oxford University Press, 2005.

"Cairo: Religion and Faith in Modern Cairo." The Middle East Network Information Center. 14 March 2007. http://menic.utexas.edu/cairo/modern/religion/religion.html

"Egypt: Social Policy, Advocacy and Partnerships for Children's Rights." UNICEF. 14 March 2007. www.unicef.org/egypt/child_rights.html

Egypt State Information Service. "Your Gateway to Egypt" 2005. 14 March 2007. www.sis.gov.eg/

Gorani, Hala. "Harsh Life of Egypt's Neglected Street Kids." *CNN.com*. Cable News Network. 1 July 2006. 14 March 2007. www.cnn.com/2006/WORLD/meast/07/01/egypt.diary/index.html?eref=sitesearch

Harris, Catherine C. "Children in Modern Egypt." 27 Sept. 2005. Tour Egypt. 14 March 2007. www.touregypt.net/featurestories/children.htm

Ingram, Simon. "Reclaiming Childhood: UNICEF and Partners Protect Child Labourers in Egypt." UNICEF. 14 March 2007. www.unicef.org/infobycountry/egypt_33288.html

Iskander, Lara, and Jimmy Dunn. "An Overview of the Coptic Christians of Egypt." Tour Egypt. 14 March 2007. www.touregypt.net/featurestories/copticchristians.htm

Khalidy, Soraya, ed. *Egypt.* New York: Alfred A. Knopf, 1995.

Menka, Eunice. "Islam Does Not Support Female Circumcision – Expert." GhanaHomePage. 16 March 2005. 14 March 2007. www.ghanaweb.com/GhanaHomePage/NewsArchive/artikel.php?ID=77396

Mensch, Barbara, Barbara L. Ibrahim, Susan M. Lee, and Omaima El-Gibaly. "Gender-Role Attitudes Among Egyptian Adolescents." *Studies in Family Planning* 34.1 (March 2003), pp. 8–18.

Miller, John, and Aaron Kenedi, eds. *Inside Islam: The Faith, the People, and the Conflicts of the World's Fastest-Growing Religion.* New York: Marlowe & Company, 2002.

Mubarak, Suzanne. "Woman Issues Basic Component in State's Plans for Comprehensive Development." Egypt State Information Service. 14 March 2007. www.sis.gov.eg/En/Women/Wday/100800000000000002.htm

Osama, Mohamed. "Eid: Celebration for the Young and Old." Tour Egypt. 14 March 2007. www.touregypt.net/featurestories/eid.htm

"Real Lives: One Step Closer to a Dream." UNICEF. 14 March 2007. www.unicef.org/infobycountry/egypt_14864.html

Said, Mohsen Elmahdy. "Country Higher Education Profiles: Egypt." International Network for Higher Education in Africa. 14 March 2007. www.bc.edu/bc_org/avp/soe/cihe/inhea/profiles/Egypt.htm

"TV Media in Egypt." LinkTV. 14 March 2007. www.linktv.org/mosaic/countries/mosegypt.php3

United States. Central Intelligence Agency. *The World Factbook—Egypt.* 8 March 2007. 14 March 2007. www.cia.gov/library/publications/the-world-factbook/geos/eg.html

United States. Library of Congress. Helen Chapin Metz, ed. *Egypt: A Country Study.* Washington: GPO, 1990. 14 March 2007. http://countrystudies.us/egypt/

"Voices of Egypt's Street Children." Human Rights Watch 2006. 14 March 2007. www.hrw.org/press/2003/02/egypt-test021903.htm

"Your Egypt." BBC World Service. 14 March 2007. www.bbc.co.uk/worldservice/learningenglish/radio/specials/1214_le_world/page52.shtml

Zaalouk, Malak. "Community Schools: Egypt's Celebrity Model." *The UNESCO Courier.* May 2001. 14 March 2007. www.unesco.org/courier/2001_05/uk/education2.htm

Index

94

95

About the Author
Barbara A. Somervill

Barbara A. Somervill has been writing for more than 30 years. She has written newspaper and magazine articles, video scripts, and books for children. She enjoys writing about history, science, and geography. Ms. Somervill lives with her husband in South Carolina.

About the Content Adviser
Christopher Rose, M.A.

Our content adviser for *Teens in Egypt*, Christopher Rose, speaks Arabic—the native language of Egypt. His academic interests are Islamic history and multicultural education. As the Outreach Coordinator for the Center of Middle Eastern Studies at the University of Texas at Austin, he frequently speaks to community and school groups with the goal of enhancing knowledge and understanding of the Middle East.

border to border • teen to teen • border to border • teen to teen • border to border